Words Facing East

Words Facing East

Poems by Kimberly L. Becker

WordTech Editions

© 2011 by Kimberly L. Becker

Published by WordTech Editions
P.O. Box 541106
Cincinnati, OH 45254-1106

ISBN: 9781936370177
LCCN: 2010941199

Poetry Editor: Kevin Walzer
Business Editor: Lori Jareo

Visit us on the web at www.wordtechweb.com

Cover Photo: "A Bend in the River, Sequoyah Hills" by
Amy Gilley Miller

Acknowledgements

Special appreciation to the Arts and Humanities Council of Montgomery County, Maryland for a FY10 Creative Projects Grant to attend Cherokee Language Immersion, as well as the History and Culture Institute at the Museum of the Cherokee Indian in Cherokee, North Carolina. Thank you to editors and readers of the following publications where some of the poems first appeared, sometimes in slightly different form: "Cedar Says," *Autumn Leaves*; "Blood Work" as "Blood Work: An Assay," *Blood Lotus*; "Washing the Blankets" *Crab Creek Review*, reprinted in *River, Blood, and Corn*; "The Catch," *Diverse Voices Quarterly*; "La Doncella," *Florida Review*, "In the Purple and Blue of It," "Word as Fish," *Future Earth Magazine*; "For the Native Dead," *Hobble Creek Review*, "Beloved Woman," *I Was Indian* (FootHills Publishing——anthology); "Rubric," *Kritya*; "Language Class," *The Mom Egg*; "Indian Graves at Congressional Cemetery," "No Marker: Fort Cass and Internment Camps," "Psalm in the Key of Tsali," "Riven," *Pemmican*; "This morning found," *Pirene's Fountain*; reprinted at *Verse Daily*; "Mariposa," *Platte Valley Review*, "Beads," *Poets and Artists* (*Oranges & Sardines*) "Shell Game," "Finding the Tooth," "Westward Facing Window," *Queen: Calliope*; "Letting Down the Stories," *Rabbit and Rose*; "Yona," *Redheaded Stepchild*; "Ghost Dance Dress," "Blood Water," "Between Two Lights," *Red Ink*; "Destroying the Spider's Web," *Snowy Egret*; "The Gift of Loss," as "Cavod," *Westview*; "Fletching" "'I's" "Shaking the Snow," *Yellow Medicine Review*

This is a work of poetry. While some of the poems are inspired or informed by actual people and events, they are ultimately works of the imagination that do not aim for or claim factual representation of anyone, living or dead.

With gratitude to: the Creator; my language teachers, Ed Fields of the Cherokee Nation and Bo Taylor of the Eastern Band of Cherokee Indians, along with elder Garfield Long, Sr.; Shawn Crowe of the Eastern Band, Instructor of the Cherokee Youth in Radio Project at the Cherokee Youth Center in Cherokee, North Carolina, for the opportunity to work on play adaptations of Cherokee myths that in turn informed some of these poems, as well as for graciously enduring a writer's many emails; Barbara Duncan, Director of Education at the Museum of the Cherokee Indian, and Mike Littlejohn, who, along with elder presenters, enriched my study at the Cherokee History and Culture Institute; colleagues in both the Institute and Language Immersion courses; Qwo-Li Driskill for river conversations and, with Kirby Brown, sanctuary. Special thanks to all the storytellers in Cherokee who carry on the tradition of passing down the culture and beliefs orally—you have inspired me and I honor you.

Many people supported my work with words and actions both large and small—you know who you are and I am grateful to you. Special appreciation to Allison Hedge Coke. Thanks to Wordcraft Circle and Wompo (Women's Poetry Listserv) for literary community. Thank you to my publishers, Kevin Walzer and Lori Jareo, for taking a chance on this manuscript. Thank you to ancestors, family, and friends, especially my mother, Geneva Leek Brown, for the "Cherokee Express;" sister, Amy Gilley Miller, for the cover photograph; Charlotte Moore, for always being there to meet me "in the round thing;"

Anna, best dog in the world, for companionship on many walks during which feathers were found and poems pondered. Finally, Mark—*odi et amo*

To my son, Alex

It runs in the generations

Table of Contents

Circling the Mound

So this is what it's like to come home

A sprinkle of rain comes across the cornfield

bearing blessing. Mountains look on; a yellow butterfly

comes close among us, as does a swallow, all calling welcome

We walk to the fast and muddy Tuck, not far from where Tsali was executed

Tears come that have welled a long time, speaking silent saline language of release

s we leave, we circle once again the mound that though plowed down, can never be erased

where are your women?

The Cherokee in Me

Cleaning up the mess
you left last night:
the shot glass sticky with reproach,
assorted plates and pots.

They scrub clean.
Not so the words
I can't expunge
with sponge.

I put the things
I can to right.
Wipe down counters,
table, stove,

all the while remembering I'd read
that a Cherokee woman
could set her man's belongings outside
if she wanted him to leave.

I keep this up my sleeve.

Riven

three girls drowned in the Oconaluftee River while trying to escape from government boarding school

The pull for home is so strong,
stronger than death,
that it was worth the risk
the river soothed their way home

Moon's hair strewn on the river
their own black hair flowing in currents
When they called to their mothers to help them

it was not in the forced tongue of English
but in the language they drank at infancy
The river took their words and carried them downstream
the river soothed their way home

Those girls swallowed words made of water
(You see what I mean about stories
they pull you along, even when you don't want to go)

Women come to cut river cane
found the bodies, wove of their grief
strong-ribbed baskets to carry the load as
the river soothed their way home

Language Class

(written on Qualla Boundary; for C.M.)

Little by little
we are reclaiming the words
Just as the land was once large,
so, too, our voice
Some words lost on the Trail
have been found
They lived hidden in baskets,
in pockets, in the very tassels of corn
(*Selu, Selu*)
Now the words live again
See? When I say *nogwo* it is now,
both the now of then and the now
of not yet
The words work secret medicine
and strong, forming us
from the inside out
Language is our Magic Lake—
we walk in limping with loss
and emerge wholly ourselves
When Cecilia speaks
she bears with her
the future of these sounds
Listen: her voice is soft, but sure

Ghost Dance Dress

The sign, underscored by security,
says *No Photography.*
Even a poem must keep its distance
as we do, perforce, from the dress

behind the glass.
Some things you don't defame by cataloging.
Even if I tried describing
the meticulous craft of the dress,

I would still fail to make explicit
the dress's spirit.
In its stillness
I see beauty under duress.

I see peaceful resistance
in the form of defiant dance.
In the dress's presence
I feel reverence.

I see the dress in swirling snow.
See women and infants, now
long dead, lying bloodied
at Wounded Knee.

I step away
from the display
for a minute,
but am called back by the dress's infinite

power to witness.
The dress's insistence that wrongs weren't redressed.

The Black female guard
looks at me, hard.

La Doncella

Eldest of three mummified Inca children discovered in 1999 in the Andes, exhibited at the Museum of High Altitude Archaeology. Asked where the mummies will be taken for display, the museum's director replied, 'Anywhere we can plug them in.'
—The New York Times

Dark is her head and bowed.
Legs crossed, arms held close.
In an acrylic container at 0 degrees she rests.
To see her you have to flick a switch:
If you don't want to see a dead body,
don't press the button.
It's your decision.
You can still see the other parts of the exhibit.

At any moment it looks as though she might look up
and fix us with her steady gaze
of reproach? forgiveness?
Her skin is dark and the scientists' white latex gloves
have carried her for CT scans, X-rays, DNA biopsy.
(Would they display their own dead daughters?
Make a headline of their grief?
Mummified Inca maiden wows crowds)

The female form has always been on view,
subject to the gaze of men
who claim what they want to take
by theft or force.
The perfect girl at just fifteen:
contained, immobile
thawable to touch.
Dead, non-white.

Yet science cannot explain how,

22

drowsy from maize beer,
she dozed with the others
then, stilled with chill,
in sacrifice,
joined their *ancestors*
and watched over their villages
from the mountaintops like angels.

In the Purple and Blue of It

Walking the property
In the late afternoon
In the purple and blue of it
The stand of pines
Fairytale deepness
Past the reservoir
Crunching hulls of black walnuts
Thinking:
This is sacred ground
My eyes devour the view
That I like to claim as mine
But know it's not, despite the deed
When I return to the anxiety
Of the city
I will long for this land
As a lover for the body of the beloved
I will recall its voice
The trickle of creek
    call of hawks
    rain as it comes up the valley
I have seen mesas
Great red tables
Altars for sacrifice
But it is these mountains
I hold against the bruise of my heart
The purple and blue
Of their mothering forms

Purple   and   blue

Sister Hands

*Fingerprints are the result of minute ridges and valleys found
on the hand of every person. In the fingers and thumbs, these
ridges form patterns of loops, whorls and arches.—FBI
manual*

When my damaged hand lay like a child in its sling,
my sinister, sister hand assumed the work of writing,
painstakingly scrawling words in cursive,
then typing, saving to document.

Penmanship in Palmer loops
(oval upon oval, rows of severed heads)
trained just the right,
but left looked on and snooped.

Caught in whorls of lies, you turned your back
to wrong, your face towards life.
Under the archway of truth you walked to the edge
and bent your head to what the bullet said.

Jane Doe, from your severed hands
they sliced skin from fingertips;
pressed their unique print
onto government document.

Your daughters knew you, Anna Mae:
Mi'kmaq mother, sister, warrior, and patriot.
*... all that was done the moment they held a gun
to her head was to set her spirit and the truth free.*

My right hand slows as ink begins to fade.

I slide another cartridge in,
hold pen to paper, press,
and bend my head in witness to your name.

Destroying the Spider's Web

I watch with wary interest as she crochets
her ornate dwelling behind the wicker
sofa on the porch, where during summer days

I like to work. The mother waits, thick
with sacs becoming spiderlings.
When they finally hatch, they move quicker

than you would've thought. I debate the thing
to do. Contemplate another trip to
the ER with swollen arm and growing

fever; decide the spiders have to go.
With a stick and a pie pan I dislodge
them; mother first then babies, with no

trouble. Carry the odd oblation to the edge
of the yard, keeping family together as
best I can, meanwhile trying to dodge

the ones that try to jump free. With a glass
of water I dash out the rest. I'll miss
them somewhat, the silken colony that was

such a lively curiosity. And this:
I hope they prosper. I hope they forgive
me my needful destruction. So much done with mis-

giving in the web of things that live.

Shaking the Snow

(for Susan)

In the night yard,
the old magnolia is
heavy
with all-day
fall
so I go and begin
lowering the branches,
pulling and releasing
just enough
for the snow to shake off
and keep the limbs from breaking
under unabated weight.

I walk around the tree
and when I'm finished
I stand inside the circle.
Just me and the tree
with the rim of cast-off
snow as boundary.
Beyond, the yard lies
pristine except for exuberant dog tracks.

What if someone took our
burden from us lightly?
Shook us just enough
that we let fall
whatever weighed
our spirit
down?

You did that once, for me.

I was frozen
and with your bracing words
you shook the sorrow
from my limbs
so that I stood centered once again
with the boundaries of my life around
and new.

Bumping up Against the Stories

Some species of shark can smell one molecule of blood in over one million molecules of water

"You can see the Indian in her."

My cousin (I forget how much removed we are)
gestures to the photograph on the wall
of my great-grandmother's house on Buffalo Hill.

I fish my smart phone from my purse and with camera,
snap a picture of a picture of my great-grandmother, Emma.
Her face swims behind curved glass
as I try to gauge her Indianness.

Blood from her flows down to me,
just as hers from full-blood Cherokee.
Stories coagulate, go untold, until such time as when
someone picks enough to let them run again.

If blood is thicker than H2O,
then the sea must be murky chum by now.
I move in close to watch that implacable face;
the oh-so-fetching lips don't deign

to smile, but those fierce eyes are cast across
to some unspoken loss
that lies further than aquarium
of frame.

Beloved Woman

Where are your women? —Attakullakulla

A friend wonders
whether she should leave.

I listen.
Put in my ten cents.

(Knowing she'll do
what only she can do.)

I'm not a Beloved Woman.
My counsel doesn't seal the fate of any man.

Still, I believe I understand
how it hurts not to be beloved.

I tell my friend she's beautiful
and has more power than she thinks.

I tell myself this also
(quietly and only in odd hours.)

Selu's Song

It was like at first blood,
the shocked surprise at gift
of otherness issuing from my body.
The first time was at water;
as I prayed and washed, kernels of corn
floated from me so that people
laughed as we stood in the river.

I was scared to tell Kanati; I led him to the river
as I washed the game's blood.
He said he had his own secret people
did not know yet, that each of us had a gift.
As we stood by the murmur of water
he asked how it felt when my pores pushed through corn.
He covered me with the warmth of his body.

It felt like a fetus stirring within my body.
Inside me there was movement, like a river,
as long-limbed corn
ripened along the field of my blood.
Instead of milk, my body gave water
to what grew inside me; people
asked if I was about to bear the gift

of another child, but this gift
was different. I knew that my body
was not for me, but for the people.
I knew that I would overflow like the river
and that instead of water,
there would be much corn,
but that first would come blood.

Every mother knows blood
brings forth life and that life is a gift.
The green-sheathed corn
was like an infant's small body
grown in my woman's water.
I often wished I were like other people.
I told my troubles to the river.

On the last day, I went to the river
though there was no blood
to wash as there wasn't any game; people
watched to see if I had any gift
to offer. Only the water
knew that what I could give would be corn
and that it would come from my body.

What happened didn't hurt my body.
I let my spirit go to water, flow to river.
As the blood spilled it was like corn
pouring into a basket; the blood
was good, since it was water
to the ground, growing food for the people.
It was my last gift.

From that dark river of blood,
spilled like water from my body,
came my gift to the people:
selu

so that some might stay

Finding the Tooth

Dusting the tchotchkes
I find a wad of tissue
in a porcelain heart box
and am about to throw it out
when I feel something hard inside.

Your baby tooth falls out.
After the tooth fairy's
nocturnal commission
I must have stowed it
away, forgotten until now.

It's sharp, like a puppy's,
with blood at the root.
The red rust tells the history
of the landscape of your mouth.
I wonder if it's the one the school nurse

pulled once you'd worked it loose.
My grandfather said he'd tie a string to mine
then slam the door.
I tongued at it to avoid the threat.
Removal shouldn't be forced.

Now you're getting wisdom teeth
that will have to be taken out.
Mine were a horror.
My mother fainted
when she saw all the blood.

Some things aren't readily replaced.
But sometimes, even with removal,

there's a remnant left
to say *remember*.
To say: we cut our teeth on hardship and survived.

Rubric

Unfold your own myth—Rumi

A rubric doesn't have to be read
or even red.

In Cherokee, the word for *red*
contains the word for *blood.*

Write your own rubric.
Let it pump in your blood through the ventricles of your heart.

It is the indelible part of you
that doesn't change, that can't be readily erased.

Wrap yourself in your own rubric
as in a shawl of warmest wool, sari of finest silk.

Let your rubric be the impress of red wax that hardens to a sheen
and seals the letter you send yourself in your darkest hour.

Scribble your rubric in the margins of your life.
Take note.

Your rubric remains and is valid in all the languages
parsed in love.

All the changes you will undergo are encoded in it.
All the nights of bitter longing and mornings of fierce hope.

Finally, whatever the last word of your rubric is: cross it out.
Distrust the happy ending unless it comes of seeing clear.

No Marker: Fort Cass and Internment Camps

About a week ago, a man killed himself....At length he stopped and remarked that he had gone as far...
as he should ever go. He loaded his rifle, lay down at the foot of a tree...and...discharged his gun.
—Journal of Rev. Daniel Butrick, 1838

No one remembers the tree:

How trunk supported trunk
How bark was stained with dark
How roots absorbed debris of brain and bone
How crack of shot rang like timber being felled then echoed in a sad report
How leaves bled red in fall, signaling *life* to men and mountain
How limb and lumber are not so far apart
How trauma formed a narrow band within concentric rings

The lake of your choosing

When you dive in, it's cold
You quickly acclimate
The water's clear, no murk
There's plenty of air where you are
Gradually where there was pain
you are healed
You dive deeper
look around
You're not the only one here
People and animals
glide through the water
with smiles on their faces
some whiskered, some withered
You feel you could stay a long time
soaking it in, becoming more whole
Reluctantly you swim back towards the lozenged light of the surfa
Your head is seal-sleek
The sun is calling your name
You step to the shore and look back:
the lake is no more
You're completely dry
Yet as you write this down
water drips from your hand
and makes rings that widen on paper
blurring the lines between

Washing the Blankets

After your fever breaks
and you're headed back to school,

I strip your bed
to wash the residue of flu.

Pillowcases, sheets, blankets
all heaped into the wash.

I think of other blankets,
other outcomes.

Add bleach to the load.
Aim to get the blankets white, white, white.

"I"s

The print is superseded.
Now they scan the eyes.
What would they see in mine?

If I say my eyes are green I lie.
They're brown at the center, with a rim
of darkest blue, depending on the light.

And the one eye, the left,
with a dark fleck in it.
What would they make of that?

When I scan my own eyes
I can't say I see enemy,
since my mother's eyes are blue.

Rather, I see concentric circles
of color that never quite did mix,
but held true at the core.

Edges

At the edge of the road
in our suburban neighborhood,
its fur unmistakable for dog,
the fox lies dead.
I feel unaccountably sad.
Narrowing boundaries
with no wild to run to,
no place to lay its head.

The fox crouched behind me in the orchard,
targeting the chicken house beyond.
Sensing its presence, I turned and cried
less from fear than from surprise.
(If there is no fear there is no delight.)
Too late: alarm raised, gun fetched, shots fired.
The fox tore, a rust blur, up the hill as I willed it to run faster,
guilty at my admiration for the stealth of the destroyer,
while all around me streamed invective.
It escaped into the tree line to its den in the ledge of rocks
where I always tried to edge my body in.
I never could gain entry,
but liked to imagine foxes
asleep around cleaned bones,
tails muffed around muzzles
as their eyes tracked dreams.

During a difficult time
someone advises me
to *work the edges*
I realize that was the fox's strategy,
those topaz eyes undeterred.
Shrewd withdrawal

until an opportune time to kill.

I can wait, as well.

This morning found

a clutch of feathers, ashen
surrounded by soft down

Sacrifice under the cedar
that my dog and I discover

No body or bones; just feathers
I carefully collect in honor

of one recently flown
I clutch my find all the way home

All that remains of flight
I hold: air quivers them to life

Indian Graves at Congressional Cemetery

Most died while in Washington negotiating treaties or conducting business with the U.S Government.

Dusk falls fast
leaving me lightless for looking.
I'd had the map turned wrong.
(We're never where we think we are.)
With the gates about to close
I kneel before the stone UNKNOWN
to offer tobacco and prayers
for Pushmataha and all the other Indians
whose graves I failed to find.

The sun medallions the horizon.
General, Chief, you served:
at your military funeral
the big guns fired over you.
They still resound.
Smoke rises to these leaden clouds.
Meanwhile, in Tennessee, to see
that other general's grave you have to pay:
admission.

Finders, Keepers

At the touristy jewelers, I ask for arrowheads.
I'm surprised (though probably shouldn't be)
when the clerk slides a box from the display.
They're $5 each. I buy one, wishing
I could afford to liberate them all.
Instead, I ask where they're from.
She names another mountain town.
I'd planned to give it to my son,
but think the better of it; decide
next time I'm home I'll push
the arrowhead back into
the ground. The arrow-
head's point
is only the tip:
Indian bones
encased for
sale or show
keep their
spirit that
those who
found and
stole will
never
know

Pray with what is left

At night the river rises
until you are subsumed,
submerged
You feel your limbs give way
as images give weight
to what meant most
but wasn't said
in light of day
Sometimes you are afraid
Sometimes you are saved
You grasp at what is passed or not yet manifest
Breath by breath
you learn to let go
and let the river take (and make) the rest
until finally you are washed ashore
where the sun is lifted by the hands of priests
You are at the center of the four
When you try to tell
what you have seen
all that's left to you
is tear and gesture
You pray with what is left
and find it is enough

Psalm in the Key of Tsali

Since we are apart, I rage and weep
My pillow turns its back on my display

How many days?
My bones contract to merest marrow

You enter me and enter me until tomorrow
when light marches in with Reason and her

armed and sullen soldiers
to take away longing with her sons

so that some
of me might stay and live

listening and speaking

What the Tourists Don't Know

He may be drunk
but he still speaks
of facing East
when the sun rises

He may slur his words
but he is clear on how Creator
blesses everything
and is everywhere

He may repeat himself,
but he still has a plan
for children to speak
Tsalagi

He may be drunk,
may hold my hand too long,
but when he speaks
his words face East

River of Words
written on the Qualla Boundary

Plunged in as we are, it's cold
We sputter and gasp, reach for the shore of the sure
But the land speaks the old language,
       even the stones

The current is swift, with much power
Limbs heavy,
I feel myself starting to sink
when a hand reaches and holds, allowing me air, then releases

This time I'm ready
Don't fight it: float
Let the water carry you far away downstream, where it runs fluid with fluency
Acclimate to the temperature, be buoyant with hope

I went to the water of language to be cleansed of conquering consonants
I went to be baptized into my true self   I keep coming to water, over and ov
Even now, as you speak, some of your spittle lands on my hand,
joining water to water, all of us part

Distant, Early, Warning: Lines

In the picture, the Inupiat woman
holds her child as an arctic fox plays nearby.
Your own face framed in fur.
Was she by chance your lover?

Bloody prints and tracks around the camp,
but white-out snow precluded search
for polar bear and missing man.
Frozen waves formed question marks.
Your stories stole our sleep—
above chamber pots
above roaches' soft perambulations—
we lay too scared to move.

Sometimes we have to wander far
to find ourselves back home:
far from Cherokee roots in Georgia,
you on Barter Island
or in Oregon
or North Charleston
(serrated saw palmetto
bane and aid to childhood play.)
You drove us to the beach in your tail-finned car
where we watched for fins of sharks and listened to you retell
how one bumped you hard as you swam alone and far from shore.
I want to remember you,
but all I have are these poor words,
these shards of story, these artifacts.
I sift through,
searching for splinters of bone that connect somehow to mine.

Did you feel a distant, early, warning

as your asbestosed lungs were failing?
Our sense of foreboding sharpens
before the knife, the rape, the kill.
Blood test shows white on high alert, attack.
And the crow that first breathed
disease and greed on change of air?
It felt a ruffle in its feathers of imminent arrival,
so flew to warn, to tell.
Now the warming, warning climate,
receding ice where your lover stood
and where polar bears cling to what they can of cold
(there was no woman in the picture, but now the story's mine to tell).
This and more: What could have warned us? Who would have listened?

The Gift of Loss

What happens to the risks we never take?
Do they sink out of sight
only to resurrect later as regret?

Who is to say that the leap of one life
would not be considered cowardice in another?

I'd say odds are that our risks
are our best hopes that, unrealized,
abscess into anger.
But who knows?
Maybe you do.

Tell me.

And another thing:
Do the years just run on
or do people really change,
deep down?

As the hawk circles,
a few feathers loosen
and fall to earth:
Does it know
(in its magnificence)
that a part of itself
has been cast off,
no longer needed?
(Never mind that its loss gifts someone below)

Does it feel
(in its glory)

a sense of loss
or only the luxurious air as it assumes the up-drafting currents?

Burning the Letter

I thought the words would be more flame-resistant,
but they crumpled at the fire's insistence.
Soon your words were smoke.
What once I held as truth revealed itself as ash.

How little stands between us and release.
How much the effort to get there.

One person's betrayal isn't so much.
Treaties signed and broken by the Great Father
mean far more than a single letter
from a father to a daughter.

It took three matches to burn the letter.
Past, present, future.

The Mountain Has Its Say

I have waited a long time to speak
with your words. They were easy enough to learn,
but your sounds came hard to my mouth's contours.
You of the pale two-legged kind suppose
we of the Blue Wall do not speak. It is
not we who don't speak, it is rather you
who have not learned how to hear aright.
What I have summoned you to say (in these
curious runes you call words) is this:
That I will outlast all you do to me,
even though your saws seize my trees,
even though your bloodless beasts claw my bowels
for the rock you crave. I will keep yielding
vein after vein down to the core of my ridge
until you tire of your quarry. We tried
hard to shield you, let you build and pillage,
but you did not honor our gift. Soon it will
be time for wrongs to be righted. You forget
I am a witness. I remark not only
what you did to me and mine, but to your
own human kind as well, slaves and natives.
I offered my caves and hollows to those
who tried to hide from your destruction.
And when their bodies fell, too weary to go on?
Whose body absorbed their blood and tears?
Not yours. Mine. And those whose paws printed
and pressed at my earth: what has become of them?
The panther's scream is silent. The foxes' den is cold.
Even those who etched the sky have thinned.
Where have they gone? Declare if you know,
you who have sullied the pulse of my springs
so they run brackish with fetid runoff

n your work. Work? What do you know of work?
e you shifted in the bones of your being
 your shoulders hunched and stayed? I will
ast you all and yet will still receive
: bodies when they have died in their shame.
he time when justice comes you will beg
 fall on you and cover you, but we
flatten ourselves so that you cannot
: in our blue mists, cannot wrap our long
k of shadows around you. You will cry
to us, but we will say we never knew you.
n we will rise again and watch for another thousand of the turnings you call years.

The Catch

Back home, if home it is,
   I listen to CDs to keep my language up.
     I let the Cherokee play
       in what at first is no more than
      volley of vowel and verb.
       Finally I relax into the flow.
          Even though most courses ahead
         too fast for me to catch,
     some words stick and thrash.
    I make of my mind a weir
   where words are caught
  and held by current's force
until I can haul them up and out
for sustenance.

Word as Fish

When they had gone ashore, they saw a charcoal fire there, with fish on it, and bread... Jesus said to them, "Come and have breakfast."...Jesus came and took the bread and gave it to them, and did the same with the fish.—from the Gospel of John

Our teacher tells us: ask for the words you need.
Example: doadt *cat? wesa*

Doadt
the mouth of the **[river]** where the blood will answer?
shimmer of **[silver]** on rainbow scales?
as you slept, I drew **[breath]** from your depths?
[mountains] shawled with purple clouds?

Doadt
how in the violence of **[love]** you fell free of your knife?
behind the mask of your **[fear]** lies your true clan?
thunder and **[lightning]** together come close to the tumult of us?
the hook requires an open **[mouth]**?

Doadt
the **[formula]** for binding and release?
never more **[hate]** than where love withheld?
ducks **[devoured]** entrails and head?
our enemies are those who know our **[secrets]** best?

Doadt
[calling] your name in my sleep, I wake to your shape?
dance of **[war]** and desire?
smeared with **[red]** paint made from bear fat?
leap of resistance at moment of **[capture]**?

Doadt
when I dream of you, your **[knife]** is always at my life?
my mouth **[waters]** for a taste?

Doadt
woodsmoke of your **[skin]**; smell of smoking fish?
clay pot held in shape by **[fire]** alone, blackened by sorrow?

Doadt
the price of intimacy is the stress of the **[bead]** on the cloth?

Somewhere I have the words to tell you who I am
They're stuck in my throat, lodged in my blood
Here: draw them out, fish on fish, from that deep place
Feed me as you did before, for I am hungry now: **agiyosiha**

Blood Work

When my doctor calls to report
there's a problem with my blood work
I'm not surprised.
After all, I'm a universal donor
who can't give, having lived
wrong place, wrong time.

When you want to know
my blood quantum,
I must admit I am surprised.
I don't ask you to prove
you are a Jew.
Our eyes appraise the other's skin.

Maybe a sophisticated sludge test
could separate the worth.
If I whirled myself in centrifuge
what would hold
and what would mix
now that plasma means TV?

Before surgery,
they checked my bleed time.
The blood patch in my spine
kept my brain from draining dry.
Is it in my blood
not to trust?

In the ER all that blood
and my hands in it,
without gloves.
How else to stroke the girl's hair

and murmur prayers?
Black hair, black blood.

Giving birth I bled and bled
while the placenta held.
(If we don't detach from former truth,
our souls can bleed to death.)
How do people heal
if not by story, not by blood?

On the Medicine Trail

Our guide stoops to finger various plants;
tells us what they help to cure.
Leaves tremble with desire to help.
After we've walked awhile
we pause and let the stories gather
as they always do in circle.
The green leaves lean in close to listen
as we begin to share
more about ourselves.
Faces are jagged with shadow.
Eyes brimmed with tears could easily be allergies.
Is there a plant whose leaves,
steeped in bitter tea,
will ease the soul's disease?
One arrives late.
Twigs break under his feet.
A crow calls alert.
Our words scatter to hide
under umbrella of plants speaking promise of shelter.

Fletching

Throwing down both arrow and bow,
With a heart overcome by sorrow.
—*The Bhagavad Gita*

The tautness and release of a life, its uncertain trajectory.
Even when our aim is true or at least satisfactory
we can still somehow miss the mark.

You taught me to shoot the bow and arrow:
milk carton in the drive I pierced clean through,
but no one saw and no one believed but you.

I ponder your purported words: *Is this all there is?*
They might have been my own.
Flesh of flesh and bone of bone.

Arrowheads of flint you prized from the ground,
remnants of ancient enmity or hunt, how sharp my finger found
the tip, always pressing to the point of pain.

Bow of your cleft lip, lisp and ridicule.
Wealth of offspring your sole cupidity.
Maybe children would have kept you tethered

to this life as mine has to mine.
Instead you mourned an empty quiver,
chose your target and were gone forever.

Wounded archer that you were,
too young to mourn you then, I mourn you now,
my grief bright feathers on embedded arrow.

Cedar Says

The wind in the cedar
spoke to me
It wasn't subtle at all
The whoosh in the branches
startled me
out of complacency
The branches reached out
and prickled me into consciousness
as I passed by:
Listen! Wake to the pulse of your life
Cedar sighs
Cedar says
Cedar soughs

what is far gone

Come Back to the World

What's important is to notice
rain drops on leaves
They are not tears they just are

Hawk wheeling in blue
Redbird laying down tracks
Rock wall flush by columbine

These are the things that matter,
that dwarf your small heart
filled with stones of hurt

Drop those stones along behind
Let someone follow the trail
to you as you are now

Light through the leaves
reveals veins within green skin
but the breeze lifting these leaves

is not your lover's hand in your hair
Come back to the world   Let it be
Let it heal what you feel is far gone

The earth knows what you know and more

Letting Down the Stories

At night, my grandmother lets down her hair.
    It uncoils, silver with story.
Once freed, stories stand
    in the corners of the room,
waiting to be bidden.
    They are as long as the length of her locks.
I know which ones to ask to hear,
    which ones not to ask about
because they would draw blood.
    (Some stories are only whispered
as they pass through vessels, through veins.)
    What she didn't say spoke loudest,
whether German or Tsalagi,
    neither spoken of nor spoken.
Just known.
    Those old German fairytales:
where letting down the hair was dangerous.
    Where there was always someone willing
to be blinded searching
    for a tower of truth.

Shell Game

It's hard to balance on the turtle's back
The scarred geometry is proof this island's under siege

A toppled turtle rights itself by virtue of its shape
Turtle shell is keratin; our nails shell fingertips

When my turtle boxed, my five-year finger stuck
I couldn't force release but had to wait

The shells we wear wear thin
We can make of them rattles, minus our meat

Give me a myth I can believe in
One that doesn't end in blood

Westward Facing Window

Having rearranged the furniture,
now my reading place
receives late light.
Awash in it, in light of what I've read,
I can't help but think
of those who were forced West.

I've only been out West once.
Twice if you count the time for surgery.
On that return flight, in tears of pain,
I leaned against the cabin window,
watching unfamiliar terrain.
Finally, too sick to read, I fixed my eyes
on the monitor above our seats
that traced our route from West to East.
We'd gained three hours by the time we landed.
I'd been fed and comforted in my distress.

Now in the blinding light
I can no longer see to read
so I close my book and eyes.
Try to imagine
The Trail Where They Cried.
My eyelids swim with red.

Winter Count

Large numbers of crows throughout the U.S. have apparently decided that urban roosts are more to their liking than those in the country. As the sun begins to set on a typical winter evening, thousands of crows can be seen streaming into urban woodlots. — The Humane Society of the United States

Every night, a new murder:
      raven wings cross opal moon,
            black and violet brush of story
   against moonstone of wide mind
         the call and caw of memory
    in movement
catch and rasp of telling rustling, flapping, reenacting
     all part   of remembering
           recounting   reciting
     their stories   crow stories   dense stories
          that sustain with dark truth,
even if fragment, if hear-say and legend
            if he-said and she-said
   Mates who are busy telling their children
        who are telling their brothers
        and cousins,   their uncles
          and aunties
    are reminding each other
that where they rest tonight is not where they're from
         (mark that),
is just a temporary roost,
    that warmth can come from adaptation,

     and does not compromise
the sure and corvid course of blood

Blood Water

Lincoln is up to his eyes
in reflection.

The Monument
a shrinking phallus.

The Potomac bleeds
over its banks

and is unstaunched.
In high branches,

the corpse of a cat.
Unthinkable?

Not Chota.
They lassoed the water,

Indians and their dead
be damned.

Cobalt

Beach glass is one of the very few cases of a valuable item being created from the actions of the environment on man-made litter.

Tumbled and rolled to an excellent frost

    Opaque, a glass darkly blue and rare a shard

Formed over decades of wash and pull

    so that when you place it in my hand

I flow northward with the river's current,

    remember months and years for your long bones to form

imagine months and years for mine to grind to ash

    and polish yours to lucent manhood

Beads

At Harpers Ferry, the rivers were
rough at the seams
with a prevalence of currents
when you worked for a month
on the frame for the canoe,
wanting to perfect it
although later *she leaked*
in such manner that she would not answer.

•

In your back pocket, a letter from the Secretary of War
let you double your coupons
at the U.S. Armory and Arsenal.
One of your many lists was for Indian presents:
36 Pipe Tomahawks—at H. Ferry
40 fish Griggs such as the Indians
use with a single barbed point
12 Red Silk Hanckerchiefs

•

Dozens of colored beads
(blue ones were most coveted and you failed to get enough):
they prefer beeds to any thing
and will part with the last mouthful
or articles of clothing they have for a few of those beeds.
You never understood that wampum
wasn't merely money, wasn't just for trade,
but had a deeper meaning, outward sign of inward word.

•

My own gold and jade bead necklace from the Smithsonian—
proof of purchased love, those knotted promises along the cord—
all finally lost to broken clasp.
Lewis of obsessive lists, did you guess at the setting out

82

what would be your main discovery?
That killing would come as readily as giving?
That you would trade the bead of a bullet
for the gift of your life?

●

Between Two Lights

(for Captain Rob Rutten)

On the night after you could have died
—*Sear of gasoline in our throats*—
We're in the yard at dusk
When the bats come low enough
For us to hear their clicks.
You explain how echolocation works.
How they are mammals
And communicate like dolphins.
Knowing this it seems I can sense
Their warm blood
And can forget the desperate face
Of the bat my father captured in a jar
For an old and fearful neighbor.
It wanted air like any of us.
The smoke of the fire was death.
You could have died.
The duet of bats above us two
Asks the same questions we all do:
Where am I?
Where are you?
Is this us?
When you didn't come home
I set out to chorus of sirens,
Knowing I'd find you at the core.
The fire of the sunset is past.
The bats dance in twilight,
Between two lights,
Warm in their warm blood
Same as us.

Yona

When I hear
about the bear
my heart thrills to imagine
him on the hills, his black back shambling
over the back of the orchard and on up the mountain.

I didn't see him,
only heard about him,
how you glimpsed his dark form,
but all night long he moves through the landscape
of my dreams, stands to full height, sniffs the air, and bids me follow.

Mariposa

The last, the very last,
So richly bright and dazzlingly yellow...
That butterfly was the last one.
—*Pavel Friedmann, child at Terezin, deported to Auschwitz*

As a child I came upon the wonder:
hundreds of orange and onyx jewels
set in the hedge-high crown

On their way to Mexico
they rested in such numbers
their flight was vertigo

I watched, enthralled,
not knowing by what name
the butterflies were called

not knowing their throned namesake
(early settlers named them for King Billy,)
or that their beauty held toxicity

When I think of their bright flight
I think release of grief
think *butterfly dance* for all collected, mounted, pinned,

their lives so brief.

For the Native Dead

I walk along the Tennessee,
Following the bend

Elemental stillness of the stones
Calm of water, dammed to winter level

I detour through a corridor of cedars
Then come upon an ancient burial mound

A jogging path's paved over it
But I choose to walk around

Something should remain sacred,
Some solemn ground

One Drop

When we visited Kituwah,
no one was ashamed to cry
no one said facile words
of so-called comfort
to those broken like shards
in the corn field

This peace town
eased years of pain
from wars fought on other terrain
with others, with ourselves
No one tried to hide emotion
We stood, proud of who we were and are

Some brought earth from their land
to add back to the land of home
Our blood formed one river
connecting us once again
to each other, to this place,
our tears mourning and celebration both

In my room when I pray
I am not crying:
I am cried
from within
One tear in diaspora
rivulets
towards home

Notes

"Circling the Mound" and "One Drop": Kituwah is a sacred site and ancestral home of the Cherokee; Tsali's legendary sacrifice for his people ensured that they could stay in their homelands

"The Cherokee in Me": The title was inspired by Marilou Awiakta's poem, "An Indian Walks in Me" in *Selu: Seeking the Corn-Mother's Wisdom*, Fulcrum Publishing, 1994

"Riven": I'm grateful to Barbara Duncan for sharing the historical detail of this epigraph in her History and Culture Institute at the Museum of the Cherokee Indian in Cherokee, NC

"Language Class": Thank you to Cecilia Magana, Cherokee Language Immersion classmate extraordinaire, for permission to use her name in this poem

"Ghost Dance Dress": the dress referred to was displayed as part of "Identity by Design: Tradition, Change, and Celebration in Native Women's Dresses" at the National Museum of the American Indian in Washington, DC

"La Doncella": Italicized portions in first and last stanzas are from the *New York Times* article, "In Argentina, a Museum Unveils a Long-Frozen Maiden," September 11, 2007. Italicized quotation in stanza two is from the BBC article, "Mummified Inca maiden wows crowds," September 7, 2007

"Sister Hands": Italicized portion in fifth stanza is from the article, "Anna Mae Aquash's Daughters Make Appeal," in *Indian Country Today*, April 12, 2000

"Beloved Woman": Chief Attakullakulla's question was in response to the lack of women in treaty negotiations with the whites. "Beloved Woman" is the highest honor a Cherokee woman can receive

"Selu's Song": based on the Cherokee myth, "Kanati and Selu," in Mooney's *Myths of the Cherokee*

"The lake of your choosing": inspired by the Cherokee myth, "The Enchanted Lake," also in Mooney

"Washing the Blankets": smallpox blankets were part of the government's genocidal policy; the poem was published with the following statement: "As a writer of mixed heritage, I exaggerated the ending in service of the poem (I don't really use bleach); an early title was 'Whitewashing'"

"Indian Graves at Congressional Cemetery": epigraph and reference to Pushmataha's request (that at his funeral "the big guns be fired over me") are from the Cemetery's brochure for Native American graves; then-Senator Andrew Jackson led the funeral

"No Marker: Fort Cass and Internment Camps": epigraph taken from *Cherokee Heritage Trails Guidebook*, Barbara R. Duncan and Brett H. Riggs, UNC Press, 2003

"On the Medicine Trail": Thanks to Mike Littlejohn for his guidance and perspective

"The Catch": The language CDs mentioned in the poem are from Myrtle Driver Johnson's Cherokee translation of the Removal portion of Charles Frazier's novel, *Thirteen Moons*. She also provided the written translation for the inaugural publication of the Yonaguska Literature Initiative from the Museum of the Cherokee Indian Press, Cherokee, NC. This Initiative provides translation of a major literary work into an endangered American Indian language— Cherokee. Mrs. Driver Johnson was designated "Beloved Woman" by Tribal Council for her lifetime of dedication to her community and culture. The Oconaluftee River in Cherokee, NC is site to an ancient fish weir

"Beads": The list of Lewis's packing materials is available online, as are excerpts from his journals and other details pertaining to the Lewis (and Clark) expedition

"Blood Water": The Tennessee Valley Authority flooded the Little Tennessee River into Tellico Lake, submerging Chota, the early "capital" of the Cherokees

"Cobalt": The New River, one of the oldest rivers, is also rare in that it flows North

"Mariposa": epigraph taken from *I Never Saw Another Butterfly*, a book of poems and artwork by some of

the fifteen thousand children who passed through
Terezin Concentration Camp. Fewer than 100
survived

Kimberly L. Becker, of Cherokee/Celtic/Teutonic descent, is a member of Wordcraft Circle of Native Writers and Storytellers. She has been awarded a grant from the Montgomery County Arts and Humanities Council (Maryland) as well as a fellowship for a residency at The Hambidge Center. Her poetry appears widely in journals and anthologies. Please visit her on the web at www.kimberlylbecker.com.

CPSIA information can be obtained at www.ICGtesting.com
Printed in the USA
LVOW101605110412

277195LV00005B/80/P